The Victorian Collection:
Advanced Costuming Techniques

was made possible thanks to the support of these lovely people:

Jaki Twiford
Nathan Lueth
Craig Campbell
Roxanne Dobbs
Luke Milton
Ansel P. Burch
Glenn and Linda Meyer
Cameron Evesque Davis
Alan Vuchichevich
Heather Dawson
The Cushings (aka - Mr. Excruci-
atingly Well-Dressed Man and his
Jolie-Laide Paramour)
Brian L.
Andrew Butler
Jen Vargas
Capt. Sam Perkins-Harbin
Paul Rynkiewic &
Karen Lindholm-Rynkiewicz"
Lina P.
Karen Bergquist Dezoma
Heather O.
Fran Dare
Lauren Zawilenski
Vicki Hsu
Daniel Featherstone
Julianne & Charles
Alicia Fritter
Jim Best
Theodora B. Inman Coyle
Nora Mai
Jason R. Merrill
Kyle Bau
Professor Pinkerton Xyloma
Kristina Glasson
Scarlett Avalon
Jerry & Cassie Beyer
Andy Kailhofer
Tony Ballard-Smoot
Ace Allen
Rachel Daugherty
Alison Mackey
Linda Checkal-Fromm
Jean Kveberg
Shelly Jackson.
Alex Fullerton

Michael L Hansen
The Honorable Company of
Grimmsfield
Rebecca Rowan
Rae Podrebarac
Sherri Milani
Dawn Thomas McDonald
Janus Rose
Jeanette
Elizabeth Krueger.
Jade Kukula & Ricky McKee
Shannon Clemens
Carbon Costume
Mary Lu McCormack
Brandon Stanley
JaeElle
Sarah French
The Wizard Bridget
Julie Cudahy
Dara Kountz.
Angela Commean
Andrea Lewis, Genie Hillen, Karen
Heim, and Carol Inkpen
Craig Hackl
Eric Fettig
M. T. Hall
Debrah Hensley-The
Sara Andrews
Kestrel
Trudy M. Leonard
Molly Hruska Ketchum
Dillon Sim
James LaCroix
Katerina Stappas and Rusty
Jorgensen
Nanna L. Schramm
Martha Stephenson
Madeleine Holly-Rosing
The Evangelistas
Joey Nirschl
Lynda Sommers Herzog and Rolf
Herzog
Neal Hill aka "Hornsby"
Maria Davies
Kate and Jason Loomis
Lori Chenault

Becky B.
Kristine Grønningsæter
Sandra Fenton
Emily Dragonwielder
Nevenah Smith
Lyndzi Miller
Anne-Marie Morin Bérard
Michele Lord
Nathaniel and Verena Becker
Debra Kirk
Michelle Cheever
Thax
Kat Henggeler
Deanna Stanley
Kiya Nicoll
Robert E. Stutts
Monster Alice
Juniper Wagoner
Michael Tomczak &
Kristen Pierson
Justin & Alli Kruger
BE Stewart
Roxanna Armenta
Rita Allen
Elizabeth D. Headrick
Frank Reding
Mary Prince
Tess Kinniburgh
Josee Leblanc Deschenes
Kathy Klocko
Victoria Kay Steele
Gina and Gabriella Heil
Alyssa E.
Bella's Realm
Ed Mattison
Nadine Angela
Lisa Weber
Nellie Cole
Andy Doebele
Michael Gordon
Gary Phillips
Michael Tredupp
Shawna Hays
Andrea & Lindsey
Brenda G. Ball
Claire Tang
Pookie

Cover photograph by: Robert Remme
Back cover art by: Nathan Lueth Illustration, LLC

For
my parents
and
my husband.

The Victorian Collection: Advanced Costuming Techniques

Written by

Laura Meyer

Edited by
Raven Kell

Photography by
Laura Meyer
Robert Remme
Kate Loomis
Brandon Stanley
Shelly Wittstock

Published by
Twilight Ember Education Services LLC

Hardcover ISBN: 978-1-958042-00-7

First printing in April 2022
Printed in Taiwan

Foreword

Publishing my first book has been quite an adventure! I have nothing but gratitude for the many people who helped along the way, from models and photographers, to supportive friends and partners, to the many awesome Kickstarter backers who made the first print run of this book possible! I really cannot express my appreciation sufficiently.

While this project was originally imagined as a coffee table book filled with lovely images of Victorian-inspired costumes, it quickly developed into what you see before you. It is a buffet of beautiful pictures, yes, but it is also an amalgam of useful tips and approaches for using many of the techniques that went into the creation of those beautiful gowns.

The Victorian Collection: Advanced Costuming Techniques looks at a variety of sewing and costuming techniques that are beyond a beginner to intermediate, level. The tips included within these pages are intended to be 'advanced' in the context that they are assuming a solid working knowledge of sewing basics. Therefore I did not include any sort of glossary for sewing terms like "basting stitch" or "ruching". The tips are, overwhelmingly, not walkthroughs or how-to's of these skills. To be honest, the how-to's are not necessary; many of the techniques (making period trims, working with fur and leather, finished seams, etc.) already have entire books dedicated to them, or easily accessible in-depth tutorials and videos.

What this book is all about – what this book provides for you – is what was missed in those tutorials, for those first approaches to these techniques. Yes, you'll want to dig deeper into them as you progress, but I have done the research. I have watched the videos, and I have bought the books.

And you will now benefit - from what I learned, from things I know now to avoid, and what I discovered to save time or improve those processes. Time is the most valuable resource we have, and hopefully this book will save you some!

A couple of notes here on the content beyond the useful tips; I've greatly enjoyed providing some background on the creation of each outfit. You'll find that you may learn a little more about sewing, a little more about the Victorian period, and a little more about me (and, be warned, my affection for puns). If you enjoy in-progress pictures, you can find many more for several of these outfits at my blog *Repleating History*.

Generally I freely interchange the words "outfit" and "costume", but other terms are more specific. Historically "costume" often described a person's whole clothing ensemble, and that is how it is used here. When I use the term "dress" or "gown" it may reference a one-piece dress (The Jeanne Gown), or a two-piece formal outfit made to appear as a one-piece dress (The Duchess Ballgown). The term "suit" doesn't refer to a suit in the modern sense, but rather to two-piece ensembles made with different fabrics (The Alice Riding Suit) or that are less formal (The Isabelle Travel Suit).

I hope that you'll enjoy this book on several levels: for the lovely images, the useful tips and the entertaining background tid-bits about each look. Thank you for giving this book the gift of your time!

Laura Meyer

Contents

Wittstock

Chapter One

The Expedition Suit
Focus Technique: Covered Buttons

My first true challenge! The design and decoration for this dress was quite ornate, and required more planning than I usually put into my projects. And covered buttons. It required more covered buttons than any costume before. Ever, possibly. Certainly more than I have used in over two decades of design.

I began costuming in earnest when I volunteered at a Renaissance festival during my early twenties. I began with character appropriate lower middle-class pieces. Eventually I created ornate upper-class costumes that rivaled those of the fairground nobility. In my years of creating costumes from the Renaissance period I had gotten into the habit of, with each new outfit, adding a style or technique that I'd never tried before, to challenge myself. I've continued that habit into other periods, hence the challenging design of this dress.

And, validation for all that work! The Expedition attained the win for the "Historical Master" division of that year's costume contest at Teslacon, an immersive steampunk convention that I enjoy creating Victorian-inspired looks for every year. The win also garnered me the cover and a 4 page interview spread in Cloud Orchid Magazine's 2-edition coverage of Teslacon. Years later, The Expedition was on exhibit for a year at a Victorian costume museum in Hemet, California, in the town's historic opera house.

The creation of the Expedition Suit commenced with laying out bolts of fabric into pleasing combinations alongside pattern #1687 from Ageless Patterns online. The clean, tailored lines of the pleating on the skirt as well as the double points and notched collar styling on the polonaise appealed to my aesthetic. A side note here: I would not actually recommend Ageless Patterns, from this experience, for novice OR advanced sewists. My uncompensated opinion is that Truly Victorian has fantastic patterns that are much easier to read and use.

The skirt is cut from vintage silk velvet and lined with a mid-weight satin, with a reinforced waistband between the layers. I like to put two to three grommets on either side of any waistband opening, making it adjustable when tied with a ribbon. Perfect for those loose corset days. Unseen behind the pleats is a length of horsehair braid along the hem to give additional body to the skirt.

There are box pleats at the skirt hem and knife pleats on the sleeves. The hem pleats are 18" tall, kind of fussy to make, and discussed further in chapter nine. When pinning a hem, always use the foundation garments (and shoes, if possible) that will be worn under the skirt, as that will impact how it lays. Having a second person pin the hem while you wear the skirt makes this easier.

I made a covered button for the juncture of each and every pleat. Including additional buttons on the sleeves, on the back details and front closure, there are 85 covered buttons on this outfit. *Eighty-five.* There are two cities in the United States that have fewer than 85 people. Around button #47 I was seriously questioning my life choices.

Expecting the jacket would be the most challenging part, I spent plenty of time on the mockup. There were some minor, but important adjustments to the length of the sleeves and back. The pattern comes with a cutout for a dickie, or false vest. I had some ridiculously beautiful vintage lace that I wanted to feature on the vest front. A shot of spray glue to the back of the lace adhered it to the fabric well enough for me to use a narrow zig-zag stitch at key points to attach it permanently.

A good portion of the Victorian look is carried by the trims and ornamentation. I splurged on a gold ball trim and matching band of trim

for the jacket hem, but once done it all looked too gold next to the tan of the velvet, so I changed out the band of trim while keeping the ball fringe. It looked much better. I'm not sure anyone else would notice a difference.

However, I still felt like something was missing. One $5 tuxedo shirt from the rummage room at a costume shop + scissors = a striking addition to the collar and cuffs of my outfit. Accessories give extra personality to any costume- I added some very French-feeling mother-of-pearl opera glasses from an online auction and a vintage hat that I had trimmed at McLaughlin & Hayes Hat Co., Milwaukee. I was very proud of the final look and how everything came together! In fact, this dress and its creation inspired me to start my blog Repleating History the following year, to better chronicle the creative process.

Covered button process using a kit.

When making covered buttons:

• **Get Tacky:** Add a small dot of hot glue on the back of the fabric as you close up the covered button, to reduce the chances of the cover falling off sometime in the future.

• **Slippery Suckers:** If your fabric is very slippery, a tiny bit of spray adhesive to the back can add some tack and keep it from moving around once you place the top of the button on it. Note: plan for the overspray by having a paper bag laid out- otherwise your fabric AND everything else will be sticky!

• **Octagons are the Bestagons:** Cut squares twice the diameter of the button. If the square edges are too long, trim them off with a rotary cutter to make octagons- easier and faster than trying to cut even circles.

The Expedition Suit model: Lina   Photographer: ShellyWittstock

Chapter Two

The Countess Ballgown

Focus Techniques: Appliques, and Working with Vintage Lace

The Countess Ballgown is the epitome of elegance with a flair of drama fit for royalty. In fact, the inspiration for this gown was an Imperial Russian court dress designed by Charles Frederick Worth. I've been a fan of Worth's designs for years, and have spent many hours salivating over images online and in various books, imagining how I would construct *this* detail, or get the look of *that* trim.

Worth, who at the age of 34 opened a fashion house in Paris in 1858, is frequently referred to as the father of haute couture. His designs were shown, on models, to his wealthy high society and aristocratic patrons. These fashion-loving patrons would then have the dresses tailor made for them. To own a Worth dress was a considered mark of taste and distinction. Dresses were passed down to children, or ended up in museums. Many examples of Worth's designs being extant today are a testament to both their quality and enduring appeal. The House of Worth, after passing down through generations, closed in 1952. It was revived in 1999, but since 2013 solely creates perfumes.

Court Presentation Gown by Charles Worth

Historically, Russian court presentation dresses must meet strict requirements, including a specific train length. Worth's court dress uses a silver moire for the skirt and a rich emerald silk velvet bodice. The velvet

6

extends into a 12-foot train, edged with a wide band of silk fringe and velvet ruffles. The bodice and train are heavily hand-embroidered with crystal glass beads and silver sequins. It is painfully beautiful and yet the design is elegantly simple.

My interpretation of this gown is based on an 1891 evening dress pattern. The front of the overdress is reminiscent of Regency formalwear, with a jacket cut straight across the waistline. The overdress — the jacket and attached skirt — is a sumptuous emerald velvet that sweeps in one elegant length from the shoulders, down the fitted waist, into a grand train that can be bustled by way of three vintage rhinestone buttons. Three smaller, matching buttons are set as the front closure, accenting the waist as the velvet sweeps up, around the bust, to the shoulders. Ivory chiffon is ruched, or gathered, at the bust and sheaths the front of the satin skirt.

Both the bodice and hem of the skirt are edged with 12" wide ivory vintage lace, hand-sewn to the gown.

The sleeves are lightly gathered at the shoulder, with a peek of delicate lace at the bottom. Upping the drama of this gown are thousands of crystal-clear beads and ivory pearls on dozens of appliques, framing the bodice and the train in a stunning display.

When deciding how to recreate the feel of the court dress, I knew that I was *not* interested in embroidering thousands of beads onto my dress.

After some research, I felt that appliques — decorative designs cut out of one material and applied to another — could work well for a couple reasons. One, I was able to find them in quantity. Two, the deep pile of the velvet would provide more hold than a smoother fabric might. Trying to use the iron-on variety on velvet was a headache I was not going to deal with; instead, I used fabric glue to attach the appliques. Later I hand-stitched the perimeter of each one for additional stability. After all, I didn't want them flying off mid–twirl at the grand ball!

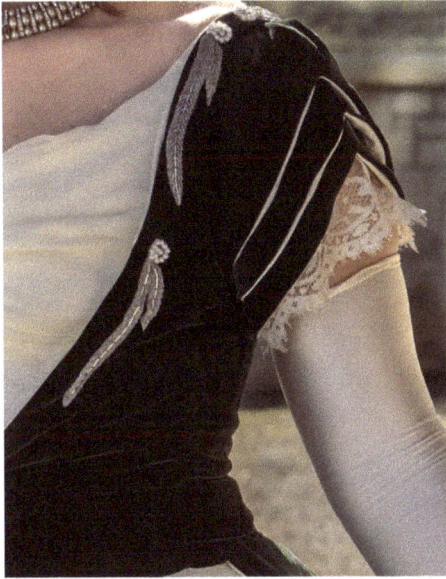

For the ivory skirt and bodice of the gown, I was lucky enough to come upon a length of very wide vintage lace. Since the piece of lace going onto the finished bodice was small, I hand-stitched it on. I wanted the lace to be in one seamless strip across the ivory skirt panels. To achieve this, I cut and sewed all the sheer fabric panels except the back seam, hemming the overskirt to the length I wanted. Then I laid the lace on the skirt, sewing it first to the hem. Hanging the sheer overskirt upside down, I pinned and hand-stitched the top edge of the lace to the fabric. This allowed me to stitch in the ease caused by the slightly flared skirt panels, and avoided sagging at the hem from the weight of the lace.

The simplicity of the skirt contrasts with the richness of the velvet and trim. I think it was a success, because I feel absolutely regal whenever I slip this gown over my shoulders.

When working with appliques:

- **Attach Them Correctly!** If they are iron-on, be sure your fabric can be ironed at the necessary heat. If you try to sew through Iron-on appliques you're likely to get glue gumming up your needle, which can really slow down the process.

- **Baste Away:** Sew-on appliques may need to be hand-basted on initially. Trying to pin thicker appliques onto fabric will often result in distortion. Quilters tape can help keep them in place while basting.

- **Three-Dimensionality:** If appliques are too thick due to beads or embroidery, they may need to be completely hand-sewn, whether they are the sew-on or iron-on variety.

- **Mirror, Mirror:** When purchasing appliques, take note of the direction they are facing. Often designs will not be made with a "left" and "right" version. If you need a design to be mirrored, one way around this is to find an applique which you can cut in half, and use each piece as one side of your design.

When working with vintage lace:

- **Clean It Up!** Vintage lace is often discolored, yet is too delicate for bleach, or a laundry cycle. Soaking lace in a laundry soap/baking soda/water mixture can often remove stains and yellowing. After rinsing, press the lace between towels to remove moisture. If stains persist, consider a lemon juice/white vinegar mixture. If all else fails, you could tea-dye the lace to achieve a consistent color.

- **Offer Stability:** Laces that are particularly delicate or have a large percentage of cutout space can be difficult to lay out and keep in place, even before sewing them on. You can use tulle or other fine mesh fabric to create a stable base. Lay out a newspaper or protective sheet, and place your lace face down, as you want it laid out. Following the instructions, give the back of the lace a light, even coat of spray adhesive. Working slowly from one side to the other, press the mesh onto the back of the lace. When dry, you will have a much easier time attaching delicate lace to a project. When it's attached to your project, you can take embroidery scissors and snip the mesh from any cut-out areas. *Make sure you have enough paper down to protect surfaces from overspray- it is easy for the glue to get *everywhere.*

- **Take a Stab at It:** If the lace is stable and you just need to keep it in place while you manipulate the fabric, consider quilter's tape instead of pinning. It's low tack, and you may even save your fingertips from little pinpoint stabbings.

Duchess Ballgown model: Laura Meyer
Photographer: Brandon Stanley

Chapter Three

The Étienne Gown

Focus Technique: Hook & Eye Hidden Closure

The crowning glory among my new pieces for the Teslacon fashion show in 2016 was a gray and cream striped silk Victorian day dress. Teslacon's story that year was set in Paris, so I needed something elegant and fashionable with a little of that French 'je ne sais quoi'. My sights were set on an ensemble from the late Victorian period, about 1884-1889. I chose Truly Victorian's 1887 Alexandria bodice as a base (pattern #TV466).

The inspiration for this gown was from a beautiful antique photograph I found in the Barrington House Bartos Collection. The lady in the picture is wearing a high-necked, closely fitted bodice with tight sleeves. The vertical stripe particularly appealed to me, and I wanted an excuse to work with silk. Though Victorians had strict social rules concerning propriety, behavior (and just about everything else), they were often as lavish as possible with ladies fashions. This is why, despite a dress being for driving or visiting or shopping, it might be made in a fabric which in the modern era we think of as formal- satin or velvet- and extravagantly decorated. When the money was there for it, exceptions for utilitarian practicality would usually only be made when absolutely necessary, such as for horse-riding or traveling. While my choices of trimmings and details tend to be on the more tailored end, I do enjoy decadent fabrics - the more luxurious the better.

I'd fallen in love with a beautiful sample of cream and gray striped silk while visiting the 'As They Sew in France' booth at Teslacon the year before, but sadly there was no yardage left. I set out to find a reasonable facsimile of that lovely fabric. Hunting for a drapery weight fabric, I searched for weeks, at last coming upon a striped silk in three large pieces from one seller online.

The colors, weight and finish were perfect. Unfortunately, the stripe was twice the width I needed. Not to be dissuaded by a challenge, I decided to buy the silk and create narrower stripes myself. I pieced the fabric, cutting each stripe in half and then sewing them together.

The 1887 Cascade overskirt (pattern #TV367) was my choice for the skirt, as it would show off the stripes wonderfully. You can see I altered the pattern to create a V-neckline instead of the high collar, but besides that I stayed close to the pattern. A basic six or eight gore skirt pattern was pulled out of my bins for the underskirt.

Because there was limited fabric between the three pieces, I cut the overskirt second, then the underskirt. I knew there wouldn't be enough for the entire skirt. This would not be an uncommon situation for a Victorian seamstress, in fact. Victorians were notoriously thrifty in their use of fabric; there are many cases of outdated dresses being taken apart and redesigned to reflect more modern fashion trends, skirts being given new life as children's dresses, or outfits being dyed black rather than purchasing new ones for mourning periods.

In fact, I drew my solution from an old article. It explained that, since skirts consumed by far the most fabric in a Victorian ensemble, often a cheaper fabric was used on parts of the skirt that would be unseen. If an overskirt covered the upper half of the underskirt, why use an expensive fabric on the hidden part?

So, after making the overskirt and measuring how far down from the waist it hung at various points, I laid the striped silk out on the underskirt pattern and started cutting. Of course, I allowed for a few inches of overlap, since I wouldn't be standing still in the dress. Finally, I laid out the *pre-washed* cotton that would be the hidden top half of the underskirt. Figuring in seam allowances, I created each skirt panel and then sewed them together. As a rule, I like to make the skirts first. This is because when I fit the bodice I prefer to do so over all of the clothing layers that it will be worn over. With the skirts roughed out, I could turn my focus back to the bodice.

As an accent to the overall color palette, I opted for an aubergine silk crepe on the shawl collar and cuffs. Knowing I didn't have a lot of fabric to work with, I cut out the bodice first, with special attention paid to matching the stripes (pinning the layers makes it easy). I planned to make an offset hidden closure, with decorative buttons down the center front. I gave the front panel additional reinforcement with a sturdy interlining, and used a hook and eye closure. It's mildly cramp-inducing to close, but it lays beautifully. Although the color choices were a step away from my usual, the stripes, the deep purple accents, and the glow of the silk have made this one of my favorite gowns thus far.

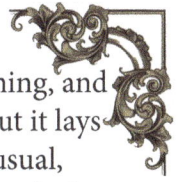

When making a hook and eye hidden closure:

- **Hook & Eye vs Snaps or Zipper**: It may sound counter-intuitive, but you want the seam under a measure of stress.If the closure is too loose, the hook and eyes cloud work themselves loose during wearing. Snaps or a zipper may be a better choice in that case.

- **Temporarily Closed:** While getting the placement and fit of your hook and eyes down, it can be useful to put in a temporary closure at another seam. I whip-stitched a zipper into the side seam once I had the fit on the bodice done, so I could easily work with and adjust the hook and eye strip.

- **Reinforce the Base:** You may use interlining, fusible webbing, etc., but you don't want your closure seam stretching or warping, as could happen when closures set ½" or more apart are under stress.

- **A Fine Finish:** When your temporary closure is in place and your final closure seam is reinforced, baste the seam and iron it open. Lay your hook and eye against the wrong side of the fabric, right side down, along the seam. Pin the tape in place, or mark with pins or a fabric marker where you'll place the hooks and eyes. Once placed, stitch through the inside of the seam allowance and reinforcement. *My favorite hack*: If you are stitching them on individually, the use of a sewing machine *is* possible, using a zigzag stitch set to 0 length, at the appropriate width for the closures.

- **Do You See?** As with any closure, use a sewing machine when you can but don't shy away from hand-finishing. Be sure to use strong thread, and consider a matching or slightly darker thread color- colors lighter than your fabric will draw the eye.

Étienne Gown model: Laura Meyer
Photographer: Robert Remme

Chapter Four

The Madeleine Summer Dress

Focus Technique: Custom Binding/Bias Tape and Piping

Though it might come as a surprise, given the color palette, this dress actually had some dark inspiration. I am a long-time fan of Helena Bonham Carter, and have enjoyed her work, and her costumes, in a number of films; the striped Regency-esque number in *Wings of the Dove*, the lovely late Tudor outfits in *Lady Jane*, the witchy ensemble in *Harry Potter and the Order of the Phoenix*, and the dark Victorian dresses in *Sweeney Todd: The Demon Barber of Fleet Street*.

The last is less of a surprise, as I also have immense admiration for the work of the costume designer, Colleen Atwood. It is safe to say that a solid handful of my cosplays have been the result of an infatuation with an Atwood creation. This dress is no exception; it was inspired in design by the red candy-cane striped dress worn in seaside scenes by Helena Bonham Carter in *Sweeney Todd: The Demon Barber of Fleet Street*. I was shopping out of my fabric stash, working with fabrics I already had, and the switch in color palettes quickly took it in a different direction than that of the film. The pale blue and white seersucker fabric evokes the essence of summer, and lavender silk accents impart a richness to the overall feel of the dress.

The bodice is lightly lined and interlined, edged with handmade silk bias tape, using hidden hook and eye closures down the center panel and decorative art nouveau style buttons. The tailored back ends in a large, elegant bow and layers of ruffles above a gathered lavender panel. The elbow length sleeves feature a ruffle, bow and lavender edging. The skirt has six gores, and is gathered at the back. The main feature is a wide bias-cut ruffle, edged with lavender bias tape and topped with silk bows at each peak.

The hat (seen in chapter 14) began life as a dark blue straw gardening hat and, once lined in white lace, was further adorned with pleats of silk and seersucker, ending with a dramatic geometric tail, topped with handmade lavender silk roses and a hand-painted vintage brooch.

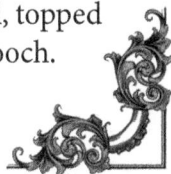

A primary feature of this outfit is the accents of bias tape — strips cut at a forty-five degree angle to the grainline of the fabric. I used it both as a binding and as a decorative element. The difference between bias and binding tape is that bias tape is cut on the 'bias' of the fabric grain, whereas binding tape is on the straight-of-grain. Bias tape can stretch, and can easily bend around curves and edges smoothly. Binding tape generally does not have stretch, as it is not cut on the bias. What type you use depends on the project and your needs. For this project I made custom bias tape, despite some of the uses not requiring stretch.

Piping, another decorative and sometimes finishing technique, often uses bias tape to encase the cording for the same reason; to allow it to ease around curves. Bindings and piping made on the grainline are perfectly useful for use in straight lines.

Both piping and bias tape are discussed here, despite the Madeleine summer dress only using tape, because any strategies or tips for working on the bias are directly applicable.

I was very happy with the final look of this project, particularly the standout details from the back view, which I think of as a bit of my calling card. The fabric weight and the color were perfect in accenting the finished feel of this outfit, calling to mind fine sunlit days spent cavorting at water's edge.

When making and using bias strips for tape or piping:

- **Fabric Choices**: A lightweight fabric is not necessary, but it is easiest- seeing as the strip will be stretchy, it will be easier to manage a strip that holds ironed creases well. When using thicker fabrics, remember that there will be four layers of that fabric at the binding.

- **Get Crafty!** You can purchase a bias tape tool, or make your own. With either, the fabric is fed into one end and folded as it comes out the other, ready to be pressed. To make your own, simply cut a 3" long piece of cardboard the width of your bias tape, and another twice the width. The narrower piece is laid on your strip of fabric and the wider one is folded and wrapped around the outside, holding the shape.

- **Iron It!** If your bias tape will be going around a curve, iron it in the general shape of the curve beforehand, and it will lie smoother and distribute more evenly as you sew.

- **Piping hot:** It is easier to use thicker fabrics for piping, as there are only two layers added to your edge. Despite the stretch, you may still want to clip close to the seam on 90+ degree turns.

- **On the Case:** When making piping casing with bias strips, a zipper foot is still useful, but cut more length than the amount of cord you need- the fabric compresses a surprising amount on curves.

- **The End:** To neatly finish off bias tape ends, stop sewing 1" before the end and trim the tape ½" past the edge. Holding the tape flat, turn the tape edge down, the front half tucked over the fashion fabric and the back half folded down against the tape. Then lay the tape back in place and finish sewing.

- **Look at That!** You can easily just sandwich your fabric between the tape and sew it. However, you'll have a neater final look if you stitch the tape and your fabric right sides together along your seam allowance, then turn the tape over the edge to the back. At that point you can stitch it down neatly in front, or even hand-stitch it from the back for a highly finished look.

Chapter Five

The Duchess Tail Jacket

Focus Techniques: Interlining/Flatlining and Hook and Eye Hidden Closure

The Duchess Tail Jacket debuted, along with the coordinating French fan skirt, at a steampunk maker's event being held at The Pfister Hotel in Milwaukee, Wisconsin, in 2012. I was delighted that night by how many compliments I received on the jacket and the fit of the period corset underneath, which I had also made. That evening, I won the costume contest and made such a splash in the outfit that I was asked by the hotel's artist-in-residence at the time, Timothy Westbrook, if I would teach him how to make corsets. I was terribly flattered and naturally agreed, designing a three-day custom course for him. That was not our only collaboration; later that year, I was a guest designer in a fashion show by Westbrook. One of the looks I chose to feature was The Duchess. As an entry piece to steampunk and Victoriana, it was a raging success, and still holds a particularly affectionate place in my collection.

This is not to say I was a complete newcomer to fashions of the Victorian time period; I *had* made Victorian-inspired gowns previously. I made a red satin dress from a Butterick pattern for a Christine Daae costume ages ago. And after seeing *Sleepy Hollow* (I've mentioned I'm a huge Colleen Atwood fan), I draped a version of the black and white striped bustle dress from the final scene where Christina Ricci and Johnny Depp are arriving in New York via carriage. These were costumes, and though I always make costumes well, there's a flexibility to my mindset when making them – a "what can work *and* create the right look?" approach at times.

For example, the red wrap dress for my rendition of Cersei Lannister, the deliciously villainous matriarch from HBO's *Game of Thrones,* is made of red polyester taffeta curtains I found, and when I needed a pocket I simply sewed one onto the front of the dress beneath the overlap. Looks a little funny when I reach under for my phone, but it *works*. If I had been approaching it with more of a long-term mindset, I likely would have found a different solution, and perhaps even done a little research on general medieval period bag/pouch solutions.

20

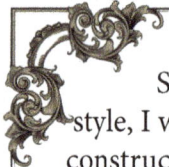

So while the Duchess ensemble wasn't my first bash at a Victorian style, I would say that it was the first that I created with an eye to specific construction techniques which achieve a highly authentic look, in pieces that can stand up to years of wear. There is a level of reverse-engineering that needs to be done with any design that has multiple complex steps, and a Victorian bodice is definitely no exception.

The Duchess gown was made in the true Victorian tradition- one skirt with two coordinating bodices- one for daytime and the other for evening. Victorians were surprisingly frugal, given the amount of ornament that often went onto their ensembles, and made bodices to swap out with skirts to save money. The fabric was the most expensive part of the outfit, and skirts required a ton of it – more on that in chapter six!

The daytime bodice, modified from a Truly Victorian pattern, is a blue and silver brocade with a mandarin collar. Fully lined, interlined and boned, the front closure is faced with decorative frog closures above a hidden hook and eye closure. The long tail on the bodice features deep double pleats. While the bodice does contain steel bones, it is not meant to act as a corset; the boning is sewn in at the seams and intended as structural support.

I flatlined the bodice, and I'll explain what that means. "Interlining" may refer to a layer of fabric between the fashion fabric and the lining, or it could refer to the act of using a third layer of fabric between the other two. Some people think of interlining specifically as interfacing (fusible or otherwise). In this context, I am referring to it as the layer of fabric. An intermediate layer of fabric may be desirable to add stability or support to a garment. "Flatlining" is a technique which lends this support and stability particularly effectively for a thin fashion fabric.

Quite simply, flatlining is the act of stitching each fashion fabric and interlining pattern piece to the other once they're cut out. From that point on, the joined pieces are treated as a single layer. The interlining is laid on the fashion fabric, and the edges are basted or serged together.

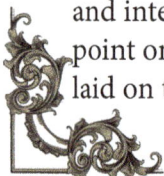

When flatlining:

- **One Direction:** Pay attention to the direction of your interlining pattern pieces- you'll want them on the same grainline as your fashion fabric. Though you want more support from the interlining, the fabrics should lay and move in the same way.

- **The Baste Tip Ever!** When you have the interlining pieces laid on the fashion fabric pieces, baste a line of stitches straight up the middle before basting/derging around the edges. This reduces shifting (If you have a slippery fashion fabric then pinning around the edges will also be useful!).

- **Lighten Up:** When flatlining sleeves, you'll usually want to use a lighter weight fabric than the interlining you chose for the rest. One exception could be large Belle Epoch/Edwardian leg-o-mutton sleeves that require a large amount of pouf (Natural fibers, to allow breathability, is always a good idea with sleeves).

For hook and eye hidden closures:

- **Stress Reliever:** If your closure will be under stress, consider using larger, covered hook and eyes intended for thick leather or deep pile fur coats. They are exceptionally sturdy, and the covering allows for precision attachment.

- **Don't Space Out:** If using smaller hook and eyes, you will need to use more, and set them closer together. Regardless of the size, I suggest reinforcing the area with interfacing, additional fabric, or even metal boning.

- **Consider the Alternative:** If the hooks coming undone during shifting/movement is a concern, consider alternating hooks and eyes- it is much more difficult for a couple to pop open this way.

Duchess Tail Jacket model: Laura Meyer Photographer: Robert Remme

Chapter Six

The Duchess Ballgown

Focus Techniques: Period Trim and Hidden Zipper Closure

I am a thrifty gal. The Midwest stereotype of the relentless bargain hunter resonates with me, and these pages are full of examples of fantastic deals I've gotten on fabrics over the years. A fantastic find can be half the fun of a project!

Once upon a time at a resale shop, I came upon a vintage 1940's dress absolutely encrusted with hundreds of crystal rhinestones in prong settings. Sadly, the dress was disintegrating, but I took it home and removed each and every rhinestone. This gorgeous dress had come to the end of its days, but its beauty would be resurrected in a new creation.

The trim, spanning the entire hem of the ballgown, used up approximately half of those rhinestones. I used a Truly Victorian pattern for the French fan skirt, and a heavily modified pattern from Laughing Moon Mercantile's website for the bodice. It was actually not until a few years *after* the skirt and tail jacket were made that I made the ballgown bodice. However, when I decided on the trim for the skirt I made well more than a yard extra, which saved me time and headaches in the long run.

When I made the skirt I was working as the head of the drama department at a local high school, teaching costuming classes and running the costuming for all their productions. I had been training a couple of wonderful students in costume management, and for the final production of the year I was letting them take the reins for the first time. In order to keep from hovering over them, I occupied myself with making yards and yards of a puff trim, gathered by hand and accented at each gather with three rhinestones. I felt terribly domestic, sitting with yards of blue taffeta in my lap, patiently sewing on rhinestones as I monitored the backstage orchestrations. My students made me proud and did a fantastic job.

In chapter five, I mentioned that Victorian ladies would often have more than one bodice to coordinate with a single skirt. This is because the yards and yards of fabric needed to make the skirts was more expensive

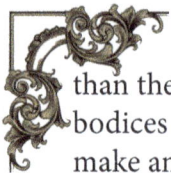

than the ornate trimmings, ruffles and adornments that went onto the bodices and skirts. It was also more expensive than the labor required to make and apply those trims. To understand this, one must delve into a little history.

The Industrial Revolution was spurred, generally, by innovations in the textile and agricultural industries. Mechanical advancements on farms reduced the need for laborers. People moved to the cities to work in factories when they could no longer make a living on farms.

Besides that influx of laborers, waves of migrants in the U.S. swelled the population 1500% in less than a century. It's estimated that over 50% of workers in textile mills were under the age of 18, further adding to the labor pool. These children were paid a fraction of an adult's wages, while working in the same deplorable conditions. The resources that went into creating fabric were now much more valuable than the human effort needed to manipulate it. Before labor laws and union movements created standards for wages and working conditions, there was little choice in the jobs that were available. With cities full of people needing income, a job in these factories — stitching clothing and making ruffles, ruches and lace by hand in a sweatshop — was the only alternative to no job at all.

A few steps up from factory work, the prominence of household servants in middle and upper class households also affected the value of labor. The women working in and growing up in these households were taught sewing and embroidery and, to varying degrees, would participate in the ornamentation of gowns. Much as I spent hours in the creation and application of the puffed rhinestone trim, so too would various members of the Victorian household while away the quieter hours of the day.

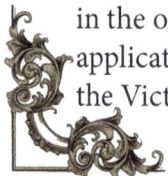

25

I gained even more appreciation for the value of labor after spending hour upon hour stitching rhinestones onto taffeta. The evening bodice is edged with the same bejeweled puff trim as the skirt, and the asymmetrical closure on the basque flatters the waist, over a hidden zipper closure. The sleeves are puffed with a delicately curved upper arm and crystal buttons as a focal point.

Victorian ladies vamping it up!

Hidden Zipper Closure from Chapter 8:

The Alexandra Suit also features a custom trim and a hidden zipper closure. The zipper is sewn into a sturdy fabric, and is completely concealed beneath a decorative panel that fastens with hook and eye closures. Once the exterior fasteners are undone, I cannot express how satisfying it is to simply unzip and remove the bodice in a single sweep. The custom trim on the Alexandra suit was made to be removable on a long strip of snap tape.

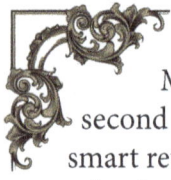

My terribly clever thought was that at a future time, I'd produce a second bodice and then in the spirit of Victorian resourcefulness and smart reusability, it would allow me to attach coordinating trim for that other bodice (At the time of printing, I haven't made that second bodice, but when I do, it'll be ready).

When making trims:

- **Keep it consistent!** Your trim fabric should be similar in composition, if possible, to the other fabrics used. Sometimes the nature of the trimming doesn't allow for this (metallics, rhinestone, buttons) but it avoids inconsistencies in care and heat tolerances. It can be frustrating to have pleats that need a hot iron set on a touchy polyester!

- **Prewash! Iron! Pin!** It's no secret- I know it takes more time, but these steps really make your life easier, and your trims so much cleaner.

- **Trim Weight:** Keep in mind whether/how the weight of the trim will impact the fabric- heavy pleats or trim may need reinforcement to avoid pulling or warping your fabric.

- **Change is good!** Don't be overly attached to the original plan. If you find that the fabric doesn't work for your original design (or has some other issue), be willing to adjust your design or change fabrics... be flexible, because tortured fabric/designs always show.

- **Take It From Me:** From personal experience, always make more trim than you need. There may be unusual cuts or changes that end up using more than you planned, or you may decide to make another wardrobe piece or accessory later!

For hidden zipper closures:

- **Frugal Lyfe:** Take a tip from the Victorians—if it's not going to show, you don't need to use the expensive fashion fabric! A similar weight fabric will serve the same purpose. That said, the portion being replaced should still build it with the same structure as the rest of the bodice. If the original would have an interlining, put it in.

- **Warp Speed!** Baste the zipper in and test it before final stitching. Sew down the same direction on both sides of the zipper to avoid warping.

- **A Well-Laid Plan:** Plan for the zipper to end well inside of your exterior layer. Even a full inch at the top and bottom- the last thing you want is for the zipper head to be peeking out the top of your bodice.

Duchess Ballgown model: Laura Meyer Photographer: Robert Remme

Chapter Seven

The Eugenie Skating Outfit

Focus Techniques: Cord-Work, and Skirt Tapes

This outfit, regal yet practical, was named for Queen Victoria Eugenie of Spain. A favorite of her grandmother, Queen Victoria I, she was immersed in court life from a very young age. Despite this she enjoyed an active lifestyle, referred to as a "tomboy" when she was young. Even after being thrown from a horse at the age of seven, she would not settle down to the court life that her grandmother pushed her towards. There was no way to avoid it, of course, but though she fulfilled her royal duties, she was just as active after childhood, enjoying riding and ice skating. Though several tragedies peppered her life, she was strong-willed, practical and confident through them, despite controversy at times.

In fact, in the Victorian era, ice-skating itself was a source of some controversy. It was a healthy and enjoyable winter activity to many, but to some it was an opportunity for lewdly close interactions between men and women! That's right, men and women would often skate together on the ice, sometimes holding hands or even grasping the other's arm "for balance". Matrons everywhere shook their heads in dismay. Advertisements and postcards didn't help matters, with illustrations depicting copious amounts of ankles and petticoats flagrantly displayed amidst crowds of grinning skaters. Oh the scandal!

By the time Queen Victorian Eugenie and her husband, the king of Spain, were photographed skating on a pond together in 1911, the furor had calmed down and the world had moved on. You can be sure, though, that any of Eugenie's pre-marriage skating outings were certainly attended by an abundance of chaperones! It was that photograph of Queen Eugenie in her fur-trimmed skating costume which, along with a nine-foot stole of silver fox fur from the 1940's, inspired the specific design of this outfit.

My own feelings about fur are mixed. I eat meat, I wear leather coats and shoes, and so it feels hypocritical to shun fur. However, I have a strong distaste for the current state of the fur industry. Therefore, my fur acquisitions are restricted to vintage finds. This serves the purpose of

reducing waste while avoiding putting money into the fur trade.

And so in that spirit, I uncovered a magnificent stole with an interesting history. Related to me by the shop owner, the stole was originally owned by an actress who supposedly wore it in a 1940's movie and was gifted it after filming wrapped. Sadly, the shop owner had neither the name of the actress nor the movie title, so it is lost to history.

Pinned cord-work in progress

What I did know is this: firstly that the stole was shaped in such a way that it wrapped around the shoulders and crossed over itself, so one tail draped down the back of the body and the other down the front, and secondly, that it was in very poor **shape**. The fur was worn nearly bare in places, the silk backing was in the process of disintegrating and some of the seams in the leather were coming apart or ripped open. I immediately saw an opportunity for repurposing, and I got a good price due to its condition (I go into detail on how I repaired the fur in chapter 15).

Despite the luxurious details, practicality reigned supreme in the making of this costume. The gray wool herringbone bodice is edged in fox fur and interlined with a thermal fabric for warmth. The skirt is hemmed high to allow for skating safety. Less practical and made by hand, twelve silk celtic cord-work knots line the hidden zipper closure. The skirt is bustled, with hidden skirt tapes to keep the bulk of the bustle at the back.

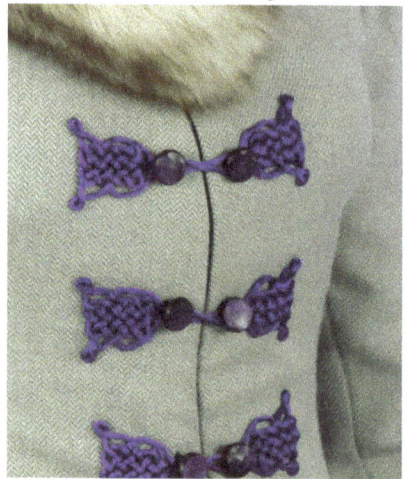

The hat (see chapter 14) is decorated with fur, feathers and a vintage brooch. The massive amount of time that went into the celtic knots likely influence my final feelings on this outfit, but I love the color scheme, and the soft, silky fur also plays a part in how pleased I am with how it turned out. Beyond the aesthetics, I get deep satisfaction from being able to repurpose a fabric or an element of a once-glorious piece of clothing.

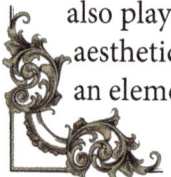

When using skirt tapes:

This is a technique pretty specific to bustle skirts, particularly late Victorian skirts which had a more narrow, smooth silhouette at the front and sides, with the bustle fabric and skirt gathers kept to the back. The technique itself is a bit of a hack; an easy way to keep masses of fabric in place. The tapes themselves could simply be lengths of ribbon.

- **Undercover:** Tapes could be on the skirt to keep fabric back, usually applied at the side seams and tied at the back. The tapes would be placed in places where overskirts or bustles would cover them.

- **Pump Up the Volume!** Tapes could alternatively be on the bustles to achieve added volume. In this case they would be applied on the underside of the bustle, at one or more points, and tied to create more 'pouf'.

- **Testing, Testing:** Test out placement on a dress form or on a person, and pin the tapes in place to ensure they don't pull unevenly on the skirt front.

- **Gather 'Round:** Run thread chains (see chapter 13) at multiple points and pull the tapes through them to create even gathers.

When making cord-work:

- **Base of Operations:** Use a solid base to work from. A block of florist foam was perfect for me, as I pinned the celtic design extensively.

- **Easy Peasy!** If the design is complex, print it out and attach it to the base you'll be working from. I printed out six, glued them on and made the knots in two batches. No differences in size or shape at all. Just that easy.

- **Turn Around:** If creating your cord-work design separately from the final point of application, as I did, be sure to lay the design out face down. That way your stitches will be on the back side of the applique.

- **Mark My Words!** If you are attaching the design directly to the fabric as you create it, consider using a disappearing marker to draw on your design. Always test the marker/chalk…some can leave residues or slight discoloration on certain fabrics.

Eugenie Skating Outfit model: Laura Meyer Photographer: Kate Loomis

Chapter Eight

The Alexandra Suit

Focus Technique: Custom Accessories- Sculpted Pins and Crown, Purse

I had the good fortune to receive 13 yards of a beautiful, heavy, steel-blue satin from my mom when she was visiting some years ago. In true Midwestern fashion, she got it for an absolute steal after seeing it and thinking of me. I took it to my sewing room and started pulling out possible accent fabrics, discovering three yards of silk brocade in a dark gold dragon pattern. I'd bought it years ago, with the long-abandoned intention of making a gold silk corset dress. Waiting for the perfect accompaniment, there the silk sat for a very long time.

While the dragon pattern would influence the direction, I already knew I wanted to do a day dress with a high neckline. My inspiration came from pictures of existing antique dresses and two movie costumes- Satine's red dress in *Moulin Rouge*, and Mina's green dress from *Bram Stoker's Dracula*. For the skirt I used a period pattern from a book.

From the pattern instructions it sounded like the bulk of the skirt fabric is simply gathered, but I prefer to create visual interest on all sides of my designs. After much research, I discovered a little post about "burnous pleats" on Truly Victorian's website. It was the perfect addition — elegant yet echoing the lines of the pleated fan shape which would adorn the back of my jacket. The design for the tab trim along the hem of the skirt (see chapter 6) really came from making a tube of fabric and experimenting with it. Experimentation can result in great design!

For the jacket I started with a pattern I've used before, and created a hidden front zipper closure beneath a decorative panel. So I pulled out the pattern & began making adjustments.

I flatlined every piece- the fashion fabric, lining and interlining, because I had decided to sew the jacket with exposed finished seams (described in chp 10) for easy future alterations. It was imperative to create the front closure, though, before doing any further fitting. I put in a zipper, facing one side of the hidden front with blue. I attached the front panel at

the far side with several hooks and thread chain eyes. I also made some bias tape for the hem and cuffs, and custom piping (detailed in chp 4) for the skirt hem and silk sleeve bracers.

This look is really about the details and the accessories. I made a coordinating hat (seen in chp 14) and purse. Also designed for this outfit were two custom pins which I sculpted from bakeable clay.

One of the pins is an array of octopus arms, and serves as a brooch at the neck of the bodice. The other is a tiny rendition of the Lovecraftian monstrosity Cthulhu. I had to get creative while crafting, using some manicure tools for details. The mesh screen of a Star Trek communicator created suckers on the arms. I did the sculpting on the pin bases, since the clay bakes at a very low temperature. Metallic paint applied with a brush was effective in achieving a bronze look, but remained tacky for a very long time. I'm pleased with the results- it's a very cute eldritch horror.

The vintage purse was purchased primarily because it would fit my phone. In recovering the base I did some freehand pleating and used a great deal of fabric glue. I avoided hot glue, as the short setting period greatly reduces the timeframe for alterations. Using coordinating fabrics on an outfit's purse gives it a custom look. The sculpting on this project let me flex my 3D creative muscles, and I really enjoyed it as a change from working with textiles.

Custom accessories from chapter 9:

I used gold accents, and a glass shield as decor on the bodice. Since the faceted shield had no means of attachment, I made a base with prongs from black Sculpey and baked it onto the glass gem. The gem was glass, so it went into the oven right along with the sculpted backing. I mad four small holes in the back of the base to allow for sewing it to the

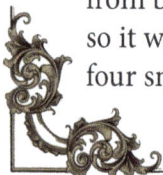

bodice, and formed the prongs right against the glass. After they baked they were slightly looser, but still a close fit. The crown received a similar treatment, with three black gems fitted into molded pockets. Once baked and painted gold, I dry brushed black paint into impressions made with small skull and crossbone charms.

When sculpting with bakeable clay:

- **Be Extra-Ordinary!** Be creative in achieving the effects you want- ordinary household objects can become artistic tools in your hands.

- **My Lips are Sealed:** Keep in mind the finish you want in the end (matte, glossy, etc.) and apply a sealer when done with the paint job- this avoids odd tackiness from some paints and protects your work as well.

- **Shrinkage:** Remember, the clay will shrink slightly as it bakes and loses moisture. Take this into account if you need a very close fit (as with a jewelry prong).

- **Props to You!** If a section is heavy enough that it will droop before baking, prop it up with crumpled paper or a small glass, wood or ceramic item of the right height… just make sure that the clay bakes at a low enough temperature to be safe for paper. With larger sculpture, you may want to research armatures.

Redesigning purse frames:

- **No Scratching:** When prying metal frames open, it's best to use tools with rubber tips, or at least place a piece of fabric between the tool and frame, to avoid scratching the metal.

- **Be Generous!** Cut a larger piece of fabric than you think you'll need. The accordion-like sides eat up more fabric than you would think.

- **Choose Wisely:** Use fabric glue rather than hot glue. As mentioned before, it dries slower, which can be a good thing when adjusting or smoothing fabric.

- **Stuck in the Middle:** Be aware that if you pin fabric in place as it dries, you'll need to work the pins out carefully- they're likely to be dried in place.

Alexandra Suit model: Laura Meyer Photographer: Kate Loomis

Chapter Nine

The Mallorie Ballgown

Focus Technique: Pattern-Matched Pleats

The Mallorie gown, my 'evil queen' dress festooned with skulls and black glass shields, really began when I found the fabric. It was to be a regal black ballgown, complete with a crown. I have nothing against an intimi-datingly fancy outfit, to be sure, and this gown was named in honor of another, magnificent, evil queen - Maleficent.

The inspiration was born from a gorgeous black faux silk taffeta with tiny embroidered fleur-de-lis. Etsy provided a fantastic black and gold embroidered ribbon with little skulls and fleur-de-lis to use as a trim. Also on Etsy were some new old-stock Czech glass black shields that I planned to use in a handmade crown, and as a center decoration on the bodice, as discussed in chapter eight. I had a lot of plans for this gown, and I ended up sewing in earnest less than two weeks before the event, which lent a definite sense of urgency to the process.

The black and gold taffeta would become the Mallorie ballgown in no time (partly because I had nearly no time!). I love the look of Truly Victorian's French fan skirt, so early on I had planned to use the same pattern again for the bottom half of this gown. This particular skirt pattern doesn't usually lend itself to fabric with directional stripes or patterns, but the fleur-de-lis are small enough that I felt it wouldn't be distracting.

An 1872 House of Worth ballgown — made with a coordinating daytime jacket — inspired me with the pleating and the nearly-off-the-shoulder look, but I like a longer bodice in general. Since the bodice would be fitted over the actual undergar-ments and skirt, the skirt came first, as mentioned before. Construction was simple, as I'd made that particular pattern before.

Ballgown by Charles Worth

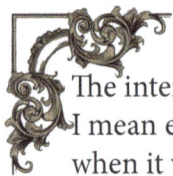

The interesting — and by "interesting" I mean extremely fussy — part came when it was time to make the trim. I cut evenly spaced strips of the black taffeta and sewed them together into one long piece, giving the top and bottom edge of the strip a narrow hem. Despite my earlier determination that I would never again box-pleat a single thing, I suddenly found myself once again in the thick of it — but this time, perfectly centering the embroidered fleur-de-lis down the middle of each pleat!

My Amazing Pleats

To achieve this, I painstakingly pinned, measured, pinned again, folded and ironed along the entire length. The skull ribbon was sewn onto the top edge of the strip of pleats. With the skirt on the dressform at the correct height, I pinned the pleated trim onto the bottom of the skirt.

The next step involved taking vintage rhinestones harvested from the lovely but disintegrating 1940's crepe dress mentioned in chapter seven. I stitched one rhinestone in each eye socket of the little skulls, which took a not-inconsiderable amount of time. It's these sorts of detailed tasks that truly highlight the labor of love that costuming can often be. It takes a solid grip on sanity to quietly, steadily, stitch rhinestones onto a strip of trim when you know there are fewer than 72 hours until you need to wear the dress.

Next up was the bodice. At this point it was just two days before the con, so I took the muslin mockup of a jacket that I'd made a couple years ago and cut it down to the general shape I wanted for the ballgown bodice. Then it was cutting out the fashion fabric, the interlining and the lining, and flatlining all of them together.

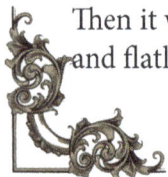

For flatlining, as described in chapter five, I use a large needle and upholstery thread, and run large (basting) stitches along the edges of each piece. This is so when I sew them together, the three layers stay in place. The stitches don't need to be small to keep the fabric from shifting around. I zigzagged each edge afterwards to reduce fraying.

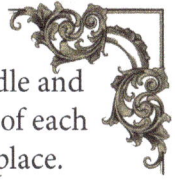

Once the panels were sewn together I got them up onto the dress form and decided how I wanted the bodice to close. Due to the centered adornment, I decided to do something unusual and have this bodice lace down the sides. Recall, I had about a day left at this point. I'm sure this is a position that many costumers, experienced or not, can relate to!

Finishing the interior of the bodice included stitching steel bone casings along most of the seams for structural support. I turned the edges over and hand-stitched them on the top edge, only finishing the bottom edge of the bodice with handmade bias trim. This was mostly to save time. I applied the same trim and rhinestones to the pleats on the bodice, and made more fleur-de-lis centered pleats for the little cap sleeve decoration. Gold mesh in two hues was stitched between the bodice base and the pleats, much like in the inspiration bodice.

Done, the night before the convention. I was happy with the look, and managed to keep the crown in place well enough to take part in a few waltzes. Happily, more than one person noticed and commented on the perfectly centered pleats, so I had a lovely rush of validation for the crazy amount of time spent on them.

Posing on the stairs

Pleating from chapter 1:

If you recall, I decided to make box pleats on The Expedition suit. Four yards of pleats, to be exact. Eighteen inches high and 1.25″ deep box pleats, from a champagne-colored taffeta. I cut the strips at the width I wanted, sewed them together lengthwise, finished the edges, and then started with the pinning and ironing. This is when I had sworn to never box pleat again, for as long as I would live. That is, until the pleats called to me once more with their undeniable siren-song.

When making box pleats, or pattern-matched pleats:

- **Going the Distance:** Let the pattern determine the size of your pleats, and measure around that. Since the fleur-de-lis pattern was the center of my pleats, I measured the distance between each and made my pleats equally sized between them.

- **Creased Lightning!** Check your fabric to be sure it will hold the pleats after ironing…. If the fabric won't hold a crease you'll save yourself a lot of work early on.

- **I'm Just Ribbon You:** If you don't need to use the fashion fabric, consider using purchased ribbon to make pleats- you'll find a variety of sizes and patterns, and the edges are already finished!

- **Keep it Together!** If the pleats are very deep and you'll be traveling (or if the outfit will be in storage for a time), temporarily close the pleats using a thin needle and large stitches running across the pleats, preserving the creases neatly.

- **Measure Twice:** Periodically, perform a straight-of-grain check, to be sure that your pleats aren't becoming crooked.

- **A Stitch in Time:** If you dislike a stitched hem at the bottom of your pleats and your fabric is thin enough, double the fabric and use the folded edge as your hem. It makes for a very clean finish.

Mallorie Ballgown model: Lyndzi Miller
Photographer: Robert Remme

Chapter Ten

The Isabelle Travel Suit

Focus Techniques: Finished Seams, and Working with Velvet

Have I mentioned I like finding deals? I feel like I have. There had been several yards of beautiful deep green pebbled wool sitting in my sewing room for about a year and a half. It was less than $1/yard, scored from a resale store. That was a happy day. Why green? I didn't have a green dress yet, of course! The green was lovely, but it was the qualities of the fabric itself that really informed where this look would end up. The fabric was heavy, durable; it was an ideal choice for the Victorian woman on the go from smoke-clogged train station to dusty horse-drawn buggy. I looked forward to the challenge of incorporating luxurious yet practical details into a simple design.

In an antique store I found these great, oversized, gray-blue and silver buttons with a latin motto on them that I was compelled to look up immediately. It says: "There is no room in the world for more than one king". Dramatic. Swaggering. Perfect. I found a set of seven in a smaller size on Etsy and nabbed them for the bodice.

The skirt was first, as usual. Since I knew the back of the jacket would cover the opening at the back of the skirt, all I needed to do was choose how to decorate the hem. I decided on something relatively simple — a wide velvet hem with a piped edge. I made the velvet piping first (see Chapter 4 for details on making piping), and I did not cut it on the bias because the application would not require it to curve around bends. That saved a bit of time.

Raw velvet edges are a mess, so I used the selvage edge (the edge of the fabric itself, rather than the edge which is cut off the bolt) of the fabric for the bottom of the hem band. The only cut edges were then on the interior of the hem, and not coating everything with mossy fuzz!

Next I was on to making the jacket. For the pattern I chose one by Truly Victorian that I've made before since the mockup was already done and ready to go. I made some adjustments as I laid out the pattern, based

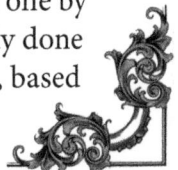

on the differences I knew I wanted for the back of the jacket.

After cutting the fabric and lining, I stitched them and ironed the seams, then checked for fit. It looked good, so I moved onto laying out the boning for the interior of the bodice and whipstitching them in by hand. Applying boning to your bodice is important, as it will help hold the shape and resist bunching. For the sleeves I used two pieces of the skirt's velvet hem as cuffs, stitched in the lining and then basted the two layers into the armhole before checking the placement and sewing them in.

I used velvet on the underside of the jacket's tail, and also for the collar and a band down the front. A spring steel 1/2″ bone added stability at the front closure. A thin band of velvet edges the bottom of the jacket, stitched in and hidden beneath the lining.

With the simplicity of this look, in addition to the felt hat base I'd purchased, I decided to style the hat and final look along the lines of a "Victorian meets 1940's film noir" feel, complete with asymmetrical, sassy mesh veil. The end result is a suit which would likely be quite comfortable to travel in, in fact! Velvet accents provide an expensive feel without reducing the hardiness of this eminently practical outfit.

Creating finished seams:

- **Into the Fray!** In the absence of a serger, zigzag stitching along the edge of seams will greatly reduce fraying. If your machine has a multi-step zigzag, which makes three stitches on each side of the zigzag, it will work even better, and hold up to seam notching and clipping as well.

- **Case the Place:** Finished exposed seams, in which the lining, interlining and fashion fabric are all sewn as one fashion layer, usually uses binding tape to encase the raw edges on the inside of the seams. Be sure to use bias tape for the casing and clipped/notched seams if there are curves.

- **Seams Easy Enough:** French seams and flat-felled seams are two methods used to encase unfinished seams. Both are useful in some circumstances, but don't lend themselves easily to curved areas. It can also be easy to lose precise seam allowance amounts with French seams.

Working with velvet:

- **Board Stiff:** Ironing velvet may be necessary before you can cut or work with your piece of fabric. Most fabric stores carry velvet pressing pads or velvet needle boards, a tiny rectangular bed of nails for your fabric, for just that purpose.

- **I'm Melting- Melting!** Velvet can also be steamed while hanging or against the pressing board, but use caution as the heat can affect the cut pile easily, particularly polyester velvet.

- **Serging On:** You may choose to serge or use a fine zigzag stitch along your cutting lines or on the piping edges to reduce the velvet fluff mess.

- **Fluff Begone!** A quicker solution is keeping a handheld vacuum nearby to eliminate flyaway fluff. This is my method of choice.

- **Shifting Allegiances:** Due to the pile, velvet shifts easily when stitching.Use perpendicular pinning at more frequent intervals than usual.

- **Ease Up:** If using a thick velvet, allow for a little more ease by adjusting seams allowances 1/16" out – the thickness will make what you're sewing slightly smaller (as with any thick fabric).

Isabelle Travel Suit model: Laura Meyer
Photographer: Robert Remme

Chapter Eleven

The Alice Riding Suit

Focus Technique: Fabric Piecing

I openly admit that, though this outfit is inspired by a Victorian equestrienne, it is in no way an authentic riding suit. The fabrics and the end look simply evoke that feel for me, and lend themselves to an imagined side-saddle outing on a sunny afternoon, hat securely pinned on and crop firmly in hand.

As is probably very clear by now, I don't ascribe to a particular process as being "right" or "wrong" when I find inspiration for my creations. Occasionally I am enamored by film costumes or surviving historical examples. Other times there are anchor points, perhaps a fabric which informs an entire look, or an event that I'm going to. And yet other times I read about incredible people who inspire me to create.

The Alice Riding suit was inspired by a striking figure in Victorian history — a woman well-respected at the time for her riding mastery. Alice Hayes was a well-known equestrienne and, eventually, an author. She wrote "The Horsewoman: A Practical Guide to Side-Saddle Riding", a volume which is still available in multiple formats today. Hayes lends her own perspective on the subject in a clear, witty voice, even publishing an updated version some years after the first to incorporate more information about hunting, as her experience grew. In a time period when women often adopted male pen names in order to be published, I find Alice Hayes is quite an example to look up to. There are a number of photographs of riding habits in her book, including one that features her astride a zebra!

Side-saddle riding provides a unique challenge to skirt making. Actual skirts appropriate for side-saddle riding include so much fabric that they are wrapped around and fastened up at the opposite hip. This is because the skirts would need to be long enough to cover the seated rider's legs — for modesty, of course.

In chapter three I discussed how fabric, rather than ornamentation, was often the larger expense in the Victorian ensemble, and how that was a

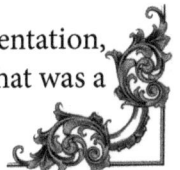

motivator for Victorians to create multiple bodices to switch out with one skirt. This thrifty mindset led to another habit of the time period — the deconstruction and redesign of outdated outfits into new looks reflecting current fashions.

The massive hoops— and similarly massive amounts of fabric used in the skirts — were the usual fashionable fare in the first half of the 1800's, and would have provided enough fabric to redesign into a mid-century bustle dress. And there was *easily* enough fabric for a creation in the slimmer "natural form" or bustle styles of the 1870s-80s. This idea is not unique to the Victorian period, of course; there is a healthy market in the modern fashion world for fresh looks created from vintage fur coats, and the use of a mother's or grandmother's wedding dress in the design of a new bride's gown can give new meaning to a cherished memento.

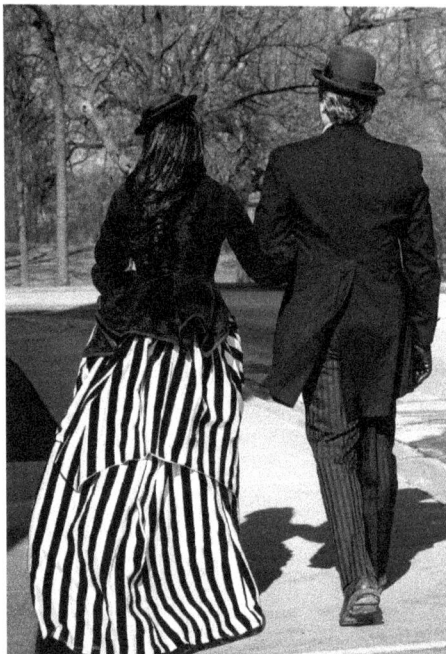

When discussing "piecing", there are a few types of relevant fabric treatments. One type of piecing, as seen in chapter three, involves creating a design (such as stripes) out of existing fabric pieces, resulting in yardage which is then used for the project.

Another type occurs when a pattern piece is too wide for the fabric, and so two pieces of fabric must be joined as inconspicuously as possible to create a larger piece. This can happen with trained skirts or large robes. The last type of piecing, utilized in both chapter three and in this chapter, involves the use of a plain base fabric being sewn on the parts of an underskirt hidden by an overskirt. This technique could sometimes save nearly half the yardage of an expensive fashion fabric.

I have a soft spot in my heart for a striped skirt, and the embroidered suede was just such a fantastic thing to luck into with this jacket. Add in the red leather gloves and slim black hat set at a jaunty angle and I have *all* the attitude when I wear this outfit!

Fabric Piecing- Stripes:

- **Go Slow!** When creating stripes from two different fabrics, cut on the grain, or the stripes may twist and hang poorly.

- **One way:** A method to find the grain is to pull a thread across the width and cut along that line. Those with nerves of steel could tear the fabric along the width to find the grain.

- **Rotary Club Meeting:** If you're unable to use a rotary cutter, pin the layers together to eliminate shifting while cutting.

- **Keep Up Width Me:** With existing stripes, remember that the seam allowance will reduce the final width; 4" stripes that are split and re-sewn together will not yield 2" stripes.

Fabric piecing- Joining:

- **Reflecting on Color:** Be sure that the pieces are aligned,on the grainline or on the bias, they should be joined facing the same direction. Even fabrics that are a solid color with no nap may reflect light differently from different angles.

- **Consider placement:** a joining point will be less obvious if it lines up with a seam, or lies on the underside of a swag or pleat.

- **Smooth Move!** Finish by ironing the seam open after joining for a smooth exterior.

Fabric piecing- Underskirts:

- **Skirting the Subject:** It may be optimal to make the overskirt first, in order to know just where it lies.

- **I'll Allow It:** Measure down from the waist to the desired piecing point on the skirt pattern, and after cutting the pattern pieces, add in seam allowances.

- **More is better!** Give yourself an extra inch or two, to allow for adjustments. It's always easier to take up extra length than to try to make a skirt longer!

Alice Riding Suit model: Katerina Stappas
Photographer: Brandon Stanley

Chapter Twelve

The Gaia Edwardian Dress

Focus Technique: Translating/Altering a Pattern

I had wanted to create a corseted skirt for some time, as it seemed so very elegant in combining the fluted shape of the Belle Epoch era and the cinched silhouette of the high Victorian period. Meandering into a search on Pinterest along those lines, I came up with an image of a pattern. I saved the image for future reference. It looked lovely, and during a fabric shopping excursion to Chicago I found a delicious spring green fabric that prompted me to jump into it with both feet (unusual, I'm not a particularly "spring green" kind of gal). Note, of course, that this pattern is in Dutch, and also that the image quality is very poor, rendering it awful for printing. I printed an 8″x 10″ of the pattern and it was difficult to read, even that small.

The first challenge, besides translating the Dutch, was switching the measurements from centimeters to inches. This step is not entirely necessary, and while there are good arguments for using Metric, I find it cuts down on overall mistakes by working in units I find most familiar. In my case, this means Imperial. Several numbers were blurry and difficult to read, so I made some educated guesses; a six or a five, an eight or a three. At times I ended up with a curve that didn't quite make sense, so I went back and checked to see if the number was questionable, and replaced my first guess with the likely alternative.

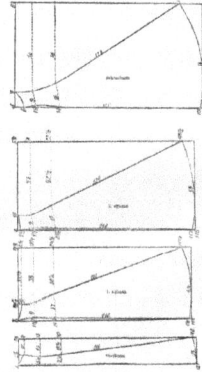

The actual Dutch pattern

It went pretty smoothly. The measurements on the original pattern lined up fairly closely with my own size, so I drafted the pattern as it was. Looking back, given the lightweight fabric, I would interline the entire length - there is a visible line in some images at the bottom of the corseted portion which I may still one day creatively disguise (more information is available on interlining in chapter 5). A thicker fabric may have helped with this issue. It's something to keep in mind when choosing a fabric as mine was pretty thin. As an aesthetic liberty, I also did not insert the

pleated gores pictured in the original.

For the interlining I used two layers of canvas and sandwiched the steel boning between them, and used a thin cotton for the lining. I lined the grommets on both sides of the back with spring steel, made my own bias tape and hemmed each skirt panel individually so that if I chose to insert gores later I wouldn't have to re-hem the whole thing. I also hand-stitched a beaded applique onto the bodice and did some (very little) decorative stitching at the seams. For a finishing touch I decorated a natural straw hat with bunches of flowers (see chapter 14).

If you know how to make a skirt, and how to make a corset, this pattern is not terribly challenging. Historically however, it wouldn't have been common for one person to have made both. Usually tradespeople had a specialty, and would have stuck with it; corsets or skirts, linens or hats, shoes or hose, etc. The modern craft/passion of costuming and cosplay is challenging in that it often requires knowledge across what were historically multiple knowledge bases. While the knowledge, then, would have been imparted by a master in the craft through a job or apprenticeship, we usually try to gain a working level of the information from other cosplayers, the internet, books, and trial and error. There are several aspects of this project which fell into the trial and error category; the lack of a workably sized pattern or any instructions, and the use of a fabric that was a synthetic blend and a thinner weight than I'd usually use for this.

It was interesting, but knowing what I know now, I'd suggest checking out Truly Victorian's 10-gore Edwardian princess skirt. It's beautiful, of the same look and period, with surely extremely clear instructions and extensive directions on adjustments. Due to the inappropriate weight of the fabric and the fact that I didn't interline the length of the skirt to reinforce it, I am less than thrilled with this outfit. I do like the whimsical feel of the hat, however.

Altering patterns from chapter 8:

The bodice for the Alexandra Suit was based on a pattern I had used before. I made some anticipatory adjustments based on my previous experience with this pattern. Yet, I still had to make adjustments.- I took too much from some waist seams and not enough from the back/chest area. (I had lost weight since the last time I'd used this pattern). Note that the adjustments were made to the pattern before cutting out all layers with a rotary blade; it's hard to get accuracy through multiple layers with scissors.

When adjusting patterns:

- **Go Big!** When selecting a pattern, use your largest measure-ment as a guide to the size to choose- it's always easier to take in other parts of the pattern than it is to make them larger.

- **Copy That:** Don't adjust the original pattern.- Make a copy from craft/butcher paper and then make changes to the copy. That way you'll always be able to see where it started.

- **Dressform Success:** If you have a dressform, it can be useful in laying pattern pieces onto, before you even start cutting into fabric. You can pin the paper right onto the dress form.

- **Hack the Pattern!** Make adjustments according to where you need more (or less) fabric. For example, if you are looking to increase the waist size three inches, it is probably safe to divide three inches by the number of bodice pieces, then again by 2, and add that amount into each seam side. However, if your pattern is tight across the chest because you have a large bust, it would then make sense to divide an increase among *only* the upper front seams, and gently curve that addition in on your pattern. Another example, if you have long legs and need an extra two inches at the hem, you wouldn't adjust the pattern to make the torso longer- only the leg length.

- **You May Proceed:** You can pin or even baste adjustments into a mockup and try it on inside out before making further ad-justments to your pattern. If the pinning/basting changes look good, you can mark the lines on the mockup and transfer the changes to your pattern.

Gaia Edwardian Dress model: Laura Meyer
Photographer: Kate Loomis

Chapter Thirteen

The Jeanne Gown

Focus Techniques: Draping & Thread Chains

Jeanne Margaine-Lacrois was a designer in the Victorian era. She first followed in her mother's footsteps in the family business, but ended up becoming a fashion pioneer. Before 1908, Margaine-Lacroix was known for the sleek corsets with minimal boning that she designed for her mother's couture house in Paris.

In 1908, during the Prix du Prince de Galles at Longchamp racecourse, she created a break-out sensation with her draped dress designs that would inspire the next shape of the century, known as the "Directoire" style.

The races were *the* premier place to be, where the rich and famous mingled with the beautiful up-and-comers. Much like the contemporary movie premiere, it became the social cat walk of the time, with all using it as the opportunity to show off their fashion picks. Margaine-Lacroix adroitly decided to use the event as an opportunity to expand awareness of her unique dress designs, and it worked wonderfully.

She sent a trio of beautiful models to the racecourse to show off three gowns of the style she first introduced in 1899, in *L'art et la Mode*, as "sans corset". These gowns were touted as being incredibly slimming, as their draping eliminated the need for what she considered bulky undergarments.

When the models strode across the enclosure, it was plain to all that they wore no chemise, petticoat nor corset beneath their gowns. In fact, their skirts were split up to the knee, their legs masked only by a thin underskirt of muslin! The crowd was aghast, even for the fashionable and progressively-minded Parisians, and the models were mobbed by onlookers.

I ask you, who *wouldn't* be inspired by this?

Now, the models were not completely bare beneath her dresses. In fact, Margaine-Lacroix had spent years developing and experimenting to create what she described as a "tight elastic silk jersey" garment intended to be worn beneath the elegantly draped dresses. She created what was, for all intents and purposes, the forerunner of modern shapewear. While there was nominal whalebone used to support the bodice, it was the jersey itself- and the smart cuts of the fabric- which created a much more natural slimming effect than the usual corset.

There is, in fact, some weight to the argument that the rise of the Directoire style, based on neoclassical shapes, made its true debut with her work, rather than the oft-attributed American designer Paul Poiret. Margaine-Lacroix sent her dresses to the Longchamps in 1908, the same year that drawings of Poiret's own lean, high- waisted designs were published in a popular magazine. Truth be told, though there are similarities, Margaine-Lacroix's designs focus on utilizing and designing with the stretch of fabrics to create graceful sweeps, while Poiret focused on primarily using straight-of-grain rectangles. This creates two very different looks despite some shared style elements.

For my part, I decided to create an iteration of this gown as my out-fit during the Teslacon Fashion Show in 2016 for which I was designing a collection. My materials were an eggplant silk 4-ply crepe and eggplant silk double georgette from Mood Fabrics, black sheer fabric that was pre-pleated and hemmed, and some vintage beaded silk fabric. I also used black tassels, a black straw hat and enormous feather, together with a purchased cameo featuring a succubus, set in a vintage setting.

In honor of Margaine-Lacroix's style, I draped the entire dress. I used no pattern, but simply began by pinning a corner of the fabric to the neck of my dress form. I draped thrice and cut once, you can be sure, with silk crepe!

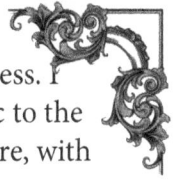

(Unfortunately, as sometimes happens when I get swept up in a project, I created the dress in one day and didn't come up for air until it was essentially done. I could swear I took more pictures in-progress, but alas I'm unable to locate even a solitary example.)

This dress was more a tribute to the gowns that shocked a nation, and rocketed Jeanne Margaine-Lacroix's designs to fame, in spite of her name having faded from the most common annals of fashion history. My interpretation, including hat and gown, focused on the drama and the elegance of the look.

The hat (see Chapter 14) was of black straw, one side pulled up to create a dramatic sweep, accented by an appropriately ostentatious black ostrich feather and some artfully arranged crepe silk. I decid-

The Famous Dress

ed on long fingerless gloves instead of the original sheer sleeves with many buttons.

The band beneath the bust was created by cutting out the shape desired in 2 layers of the fashion fabric, using iron on interfacing to add sturdiness and sewing them together. I turned them right side out and pressed the band, using an embroidery stitch to embellish the edges. I tacked the band to the seams and hand-stitched it at the center and back.

Instead of creating a muslin underskirt, I inserted the pleated sheer fabric into the side slits of the skirt, and that worked very well. True to the original aesthetic, this dress is indeed "sans corset". In fact, it is even a bit more daring, as there is no silk jersey undergarment for the bodice. I love this dress, as it manages to feel luxurious, stylish and risque all at once.

Jeanne Gown model: Madison Linn Knabe
Photographer: Laura Meyer

Thread Chains:

There are a couple places on this dress where I utilized thread chains. Thread chains can attach snaps to keep bra straps in place, attach a hem to lining, keep swags of fabric from shifting, etc. They might be used instead of a strap or ribbon, when the former would be too bulky or add unnecessary stitching to a project.

A thread chain is created by holding a looped thread with one hand, pulling the same thread through that loop, and pulling the first loop closed as you create a loop with the thread you just pulled through the first one. And repeat as often as necessary. Thread chains can be delicate or imposing depending on the weight of thread used, according to your needs, but are always sturdy.

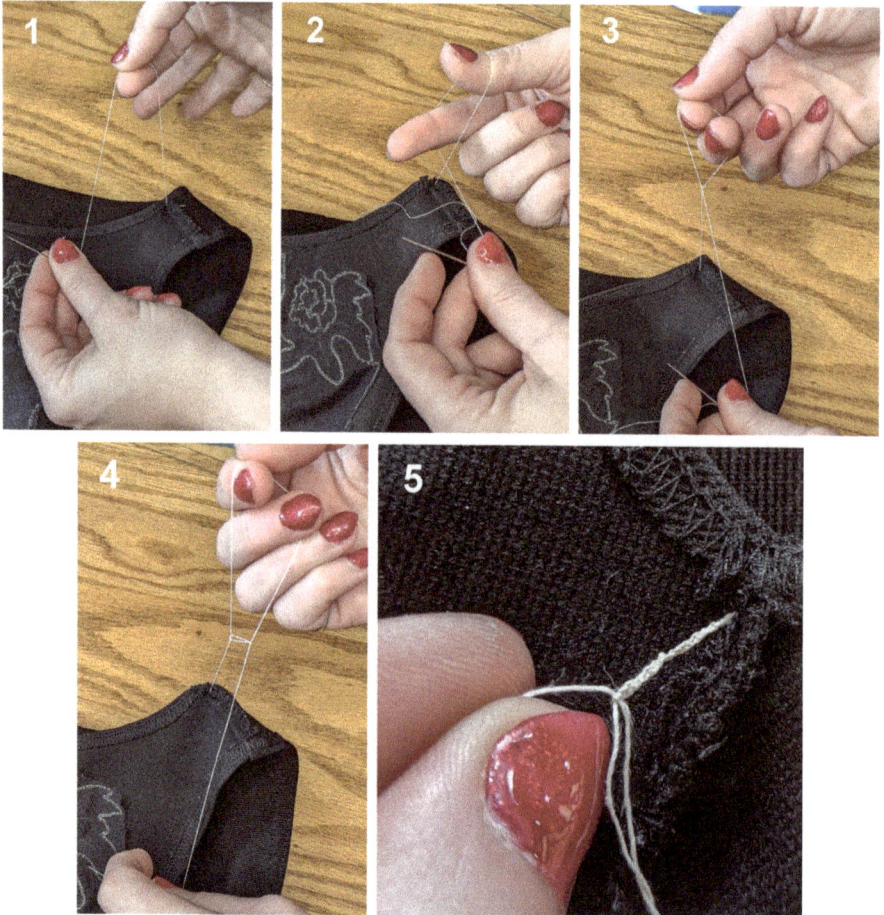

When draping:

- **Prep the Stage:** Make sure the correct measurements are set on your dress form, reflecting the size with any undergarments you plan to wear with the finished item, and the correct height with shoes on. You may find it useful to mark with dressmakers tape (or painter's tape, or pinned on thread/ribbons) important place markers such as: waist, mid-bust, princess seams, etc.

- **Stock Up!** Ensure you have more than enough fabric. This seems obvious, but really, especially if you're draping on the bias, make sure you have more than enough fabric!

- **All in Good Time:** Work in sections. This will depend on what you're making, but you may drape the front section first, or the bodice, or the skirt, or a sleeve. Focus on one area at a time.

- **Moving Right Along:** As you complete sections, baste the pieces (with seam allowances lined up) on the dress form. This will allow you to eventually remove it, try it on, and if necessary return it to the dress form before stitching.

Chapter Fourteen

Millinery Tips

Focus Looks from Chapters 4, 8, 12 and 13

I find that hats add a unique voice to an outfit, but many costumers find them intimidating- rightly so, as hatmaking and millinery decoration are both skilled professions in their own rights. I have made and customized hats for a number of my designs, and have some helpful tips for anyone looking to add a dapper topper to any costume!

I regularly travel the full millinery spectrum from recovering or decorating existing hats, to beginning with felt or straw bases and designing from there, to creating a completely new construction from buckram. I have stitched and I have glued, and I have hot-glued. I am not here to tell you that one material is better than the other, but only to tell you how I achieved results according to my specific needs, and how you can avoid possible snags in similar situations. I have had a lot of success with using straw hat bases, considering the scale (Belle Epoch) of the looks I have wanted to achieve. Straw provides strength and a textured surface that is easy to work with.

Chapter 4- The Madeleine Summer Dress hat

The Madeleine was a look in which I wanted to achieve a "pastel parasol" feel using a minimum of confection-inspired ruffles that tend to be so common on summery Victorian dresses. I tend to like a tailored, structured look, so this was a challenge. I used the hat as a focal point, and created interest with folds and angles.

The underside is covered in lace. I hand-stitched a rectangle along the edge, then evenly pinned, gathered and stitched it to the base of the crown interior. After pleating strips of coordinating fabrics, I stitched the layers of pleats to the brim and added some dots of hot glue to keep them from turning up in the wind. I used a triangle, folded and ironed to create diamonds, and centered it at the back. I tacked one edge of the brim up to show off the lace.

- **Hair Today…** Plastic hair combs sewn into the crown can help keep a heavy hat in place, but test placement first.

- **Shine On**: Avoid using hot glue with sheer or semi-sheer fabrics; the shine of the glue will show.

- **No Take-Backs!** Test fabric glue on a bit of your fabric before decorating your hat— it can soak through and show discoloration even after drying.

  Note- Using water-based glue in hat-making has other draw backs. Keep this in mind when wearing any such hat in the rain, and also be extraordinarily careful with spot-cleaning it.

Chapter 8- The Alexandra Suit hat

I began with a purchased felt hat base in the desired shape. It was being advertised as a finished hat with a black ribbon and a piece of netting hot-glued onto the gray felt base. The hot-glued bits were removed and a pattern was created from it to cover it in satin. I added a length of millinery wire to the edge as well. After the covering was on, it was really just draping some gold fabric and curling the 10 ostrich feathers. I sculpted a Cthulhu pin from bakeable clay (see chapter 8), and after everything else was done I added a couple thread chain loops at the sides for securing the hat with bobby pins (see Chapter 13).

- **Wrap it Up**! If you don't have millinery wire, regular wire of a workable gauge can be wrapped in florist's tape or even duct tape. The wrapping keeps it from shifting in place from where you stitch it on.

- **Crowning Glory:** When recovering a hat in this manner, it's easiest to work in sections- stitch the crown oval on, then the crown shape, then the brim, etc. Each new section covers over the stitches from the last one.

- **Safe and Secure:** Thread chains or short lengths or ribbon stitched on at the hat band provide a place for bobby pins to secure to.

Chapter 12- The Gaia Dress hat

This was another summery look that began with a large straw hat. I wanted to create a "Garden Party" hat, so bought a small armful of green and white artificial flowers. I took the green striped fabric of the dress and made a band for the base of the crown, and a bias tape strip for around the brim edge. Besides the bias tape and a couple swaths of green and white organza, it was just me and a glue gun for this one — it was fast and quite fun! I added a tiny wired hummingbird made of feathers to hover over the flowers. Very summery!

- **A Little Biased:** A bias tape band around the edge of the rim can usually be machine-stitched on, with pinning and patience, and is an alternative to the finished edge shown from the Alexandra Suit finished brim edge.

- **Forehead Forethought:** While a grosgrain ribbon stitched at the base of the crown is better than no hatband at all, it will still leave marks on your skin. A hat band with more padding will be gentler on you.

- **Glue it!** When using artificial flowers, inspect the construction; you may need to add some glue to the center of layered flowers to ensure they don't come apart after attaching them to your hat.

- **So-so Visible:** Stitching flowers on is an alternative to glue, though the glue holds very well to straw. If stitching, avoid so-called 'invisible thread' which is actually plastic and reflects light, rendering it very much visible!

Chapter 13- The Jeanne Gown hat

There are several hats I've made that did *not* start with a wide-brimmed straw hat; the one made for the Eugenie Skating Outfit was built up from a small straw base, the hat for the Étienne Gown was a redesign using a 1950's felt hat, and the Isabelle Travel Suit was an asymmetric felt base styled with a 1940's feel. But the last creation here — also from straw — is the wildly dramatic black and aubergine creation for the Jeanne Margaine-Lacroix inspired dress (chapter 13).

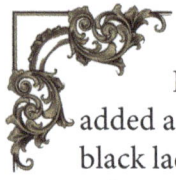

For this hat I pinned one side up nearly as high as it could go, and added a number of trimmings around the crown: a wide band of beaded black lace, a large rosette of vintage black pleating, a loose gather of aubergine silk around an onyx pin, and a nearly two-foot long, swooping black ostrich feather. I used primarily hot glue for affixing the trims, but the feather needed additional support to maintain its position. It was low-work and high-drama, and that's all I can ask for sometimes.

- **Drip-Dry:** Some dyed straw hats are not water safe- check the tag if there is one, or water test an inconspicuous area if you're unsure.

- **Call for Reinforcements!** You can stitch covered wire *or* sewable plastic boning along the base of a felt hat to provide more structure. Just be sure to line it with a hatband so it is still comfortable enough to wear.

- **So Tired:** Sometimes vintage felt hats want to collapse no matter what. The same boning can reinforce the crown if crisscrossed in an X under the crown. Again, cover any edges for comfort.

- **The Feather is a Lie!** Stitching a piece of wire to the shaft of a feather can provide artificial support, or keep it where you want it- use paint or a marker to blend the wire to the color of the feather.

Chapter Fifteen

Fur and Leather

Focus Looks from Chapters 7 and 11

Focus Feature: Victorian Mantle and Muff Set

In chapter seven I talked a bit about fur, my feelings about it and why and how I choose to use it in my costuming. I feel there are a number of valid reasons to avoid supporting the international fur trade, as it stands. But whether you make efforts to acquire vintage pieces as I do, buy ethically sourced fur, or use faux fur, please know that many of the tips about sewing with fur can be applied to all of those things.

My working knowledge of leather is less than that of fur, but most of the following tips can also be applied to many faux suede and 'pleather' (artificial leather) fabrics.

The fur mantle and muff:

This was made as an in-character addition to the Duchess ensemble for Tesla-con one year. I'd taken a slow, lighthearted approach to building any sort of steampunk 'character'. My interest in costuming around the Victorian era is primarily sartorial. While I definitely enjoy Steampunk music, aesthetics, etc, my focus is on the clothing design. But this Victorian mantle and muff set was the first piece that I made as part of this character I was very slowly developing.

The mantle, perfect for a preposterously fancy lady from French Canada, is created from a long white rabbit fur coat with black dyed accents to look like ermine. (Ermine tails trim the fur lining of many royal outfits in photographs and paintings throughout history.) I managed to find someone who had a small bunch of "new old-stock" tails in a massive off-selling of their grandparents' attic.

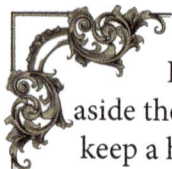

I created the shape of the mantle first, cutting it out and setting aside the fur I would use for the muff. As when working with velvet, I keep a handheld vacuum or roll of tape nearby to catch flyaway fluff. The first order of business whenever I'm working with vintage fur is to inspect the back. You *can* look by separating the fur from the outside, and you'll definitely see any bare spots or rips, but you get a much better idea of the overall condition from the back. Usually this involves removing lining and batting/padding. At that point you can tell if the leather base is dry and cracking, if it is particularly thin or worn, the integrity of any joined seams, etc. It's at this point that I determine if any repairs need to be done.

This fur was in good condition so I replaced the batting and chose a lining. Since it was made to match the Duchess outfit, I lined both the mantle and the muff with the same royal blue taffeta used in the gown. They are decorated with the ermine tails, vintage crystal buttons and a blue satin bow.

The end result was a set fit for nobility, and very fitting for the Latin motto I had chosen to adorn the "family crest" I made…. "Apertissime Opulenta", loosely translated to "Quite Obviously Wealthy".

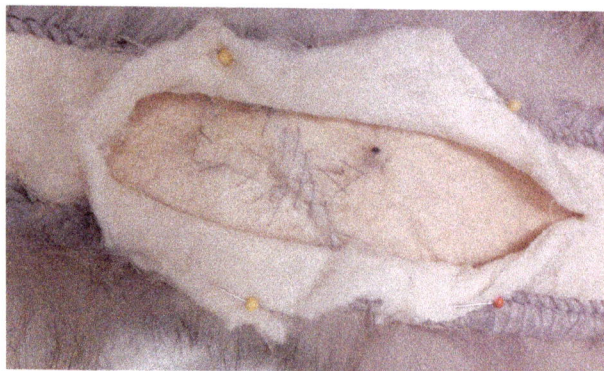

Fur repair from the back

Chapter 7- The Eugenie Skating Outfit:

In chapter seven I delved into the background of the long fur stole I found for the skating outfit. What I did *not* get into was the poor condition of the fur. There were worn areas, rubbed down to nearly bare, there were tears in the fur, and there was evidence of water stains on the lining. However, there was no telltale scent of mold coming off the fur, so that gave me hope. After removing the lining and padding, I made some repairs, cut some areas out, and strengthened a couple weak points.

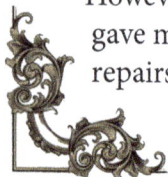

Chapter 11- The Alice Riding Suit:

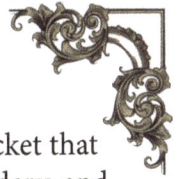

The Alice Riding Suit, in chapter 11, features a stunning jacket that I did *not* make from scratch. It is a suede jacket with black embroidery, and began life as a winter coat I found in a resale store. I believe I've expounded on my love of giving vintage finds new life. The size was very close to what I needed, after removing the lining and insulation. Essentially I just re-shaped the existing coat to fit a corseted shape. I knew embroidered leather was beyond my skill set; self-awareness of your strengths *and* your limits is a useful part of the costuming process. However, I did learn a couple of important points about sewing leather in the process of reshaping this coat.

Working with fur:

- **Out of the Way!** When preparing to cut fur, have someone hold the fur back from both sides, allowing the cut to be more even.

- **Brush it Back:** When sewing fur, use a zipper foot, keep the stitch length to about 9 per inch, and again try to brush the fur back from the stitching area. A piece of interfacing could be used to avoid stretching or slipping while sewing.

- **Away from the Edge!** To close a tear in fur, hand-sew large, crisscrossing stitches (similar to darning). To avoid damaging the leather further, don't stitch too close to the edges.

- **Take it to the Base:** If the base leather is too damaged or fragile to sew, consider reinforcing it with a natural fiber fabric backing, adhered with Leathercraft cement, rubber cement or another appropriate glue.

- **A Light Touch:** Use a round-ended 'gloving' needle to gently pull caught fur from seams.

- **De-furred Interest:** When lapping seams, remove the fur from about a half inch along one side for the seam allowance.

Working with leather:

- **The FundamEntals:** Make sure you're using a leather needle, appropriate weight thread, and long stitches.

- **It's the Clamp!** Tiny clamps or clothespins are a good way to keep leather from shifting while sewing without damaging it with pins.

- **Don't Over-stretch:** Leather can have a tendency to pull and stretch beneath the presser foot. Consider using a walking foot when machine sewing, or hand sewing.

Token Victorian Gentleman: James Opalewski

Bibliography

Blum, Stella. *Victorian Fashions and Costumes from Harper's Bazar: 1867-1898*. Dover, 1974.

Gernsheim, Alison. *Victorian and Edwardian Fashion: A Photographic Survey*. Dover, 1981.

Harris, Kristina. *Authentic Victorian Fashion Patterns: A Complete Lady's Wardrobe*. Dover, 1999.

Johnston, Lucy, et al. *Nineteenth Century Fashion in Detail*. V & A Publishing, 2009.

MS, Heather. "What Is a Burnouse Pleat?" Truly Victorian, 30 July 2021, https://trulyvictorian.info/index.php/2021/07/30/what-is-a-burnouse-pleat/.
*Note- this is not the original article published in 2014.

Rbkclibraries. "Margaine-Lacroix and the Dresses That Shocked Paris." Rbkc Libraries Blog, 19 July 2013, https://rbkclibraries.wordpress.com/2013/07/12/margaine-lacroix-and-the-dresses-that-shocked-paris/

Salen, Jill. *Corsets: Historic Patterns and Techniques*. Costume & Fashion Press, 2008.

Seleshanko, Kristina. *Authentic Victorian Dressmaking Techniques*. Dover Publications, 1999.

Sobel, Sharon. *Draping Period Costumes: Classical Greek to Victorian*. New York, 2013.

Takeda, Sharon Sadako, et al. *Fashioning Fashion: European Dress in Detail, 1700-1915*. Los Angeles County Museum of Art, 2012.

Laura Meyer believes that life is as much of an event as you make it, and she's here to fance it up. A writer, educator and designer for over two decades, Laura has also spent years teaching, giving presentations and demonstrations on Victorian-era fashion and undergarments, among other topics.

She holds multiple degrees from Alverno College, including a masters in Education. Operating as Twilight Attire since 2001, in 2021 she officially launched Twilight Ember Education Services, LLC, to serve as an umbrella company covering her product lines as well as educational offerings.

Over the last two decades she has hosted and participated in numerous art and fashion shows, flexing her 2D art muscles beyond the usual textile creations. When the boss allows her free time, she enjoys reading, PC gaming, camping, inconsistently dropping blurbs into her blog *Repleating History*, and giving lots of attention to her furry boy Garrus (without neglecting other, less furry boys).

Art by Nathan Lueth Illustration LLC